Letters to Barbara

By
Mary Croft

Letters to Barbara

By

Mary Croft

Letters to Barbara
Copyright © 2016 Mary Croft. Produced and printed by Stillwater River Publications. All rights reserved. Written and produced in the United States of America. This book may not be reproduced or sold in any form without the expressed, written permission of the authors and publisher.

Visit our website at **www.StillwaterPress.com** for more information.

First Stillwater River Publications Edition

ISBN-10: 0-692-62217-9
ISBN-13: 978-069262217-9

1 2 3 4 5 6 7 8 9 10
Written by Mary Croft
All photographs including cover photo from the Croft Family Collection
Cover design by Dawn M. Porter
Published by Stillwater River Publications, Glocester, RI, USA

Dedication

This book is dedicated to the memory of

Nancy A. Croft

Agnes Sharpe Mahar

Thomas Mahar, Sr.

Euphemia Sharpe-Donovan

Thomas Mahar, Jr.

Dorothy Mahar Sherburne

James Mahar

Barbara A. Mahar

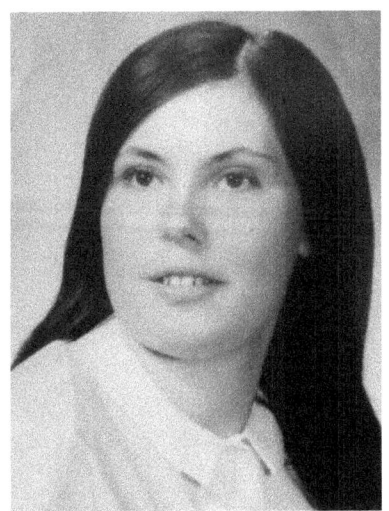

Sheila Mahar Clark

John Christopher Sherburne

Table of Contents

From Fairy Tale to Adventure Story.......3

The Journey Begins............................28

What's It All About............................37

Remembering My Grandmother..........52

Memories of My Father........................59

Mother's Day......................................75

Nancy..90

Good Grief!.......................................102

Examples..115

Thank You..118

About the Author..............................119

Introduction

Grief is something we experience as a result of the losses we encounter. It not only occurs as the result of death, but happens regularly as a reaction to various situations. Unfulfilled dreams, disappointments, aging, and illness are just a few of the situations that cause feelings of loss. To deny loss and to fail to grieve it is to deprive yourself of your journey; however, by embracing your grief and processing it, you can improve the quality and direction of your life.

This book is an account of the many losses in my life. It is about my futile efforts to run away from them, and it is about the freedom I attained once I learned that accepting and grieving the losses could lead me into myself rather than away from myself.

Grieving your losses allows you to develop fully. Whether you choose to grieve or not to grieve could have an impact on the quality of your life. Every day we automatically evolve and change and our spirits react to that change; but it requires a conscious effort to embark on the process of grieving which is what Letters to Barbara is all about.

The book was born out of my personal experience with the process of grieving and out of my belief that all good things deserve to be shared. My hope is that, when I am no longer on this beautiful Earth, my truth will remain with my children and grandchildren and their children so that they will know of the journey I traveled and how part of their legacy developed. It is my wish that they will choose to live and love their lives to the fullest by recognizing, accepting, and grieving their losses.

From Fairy Tale To Adventure Story

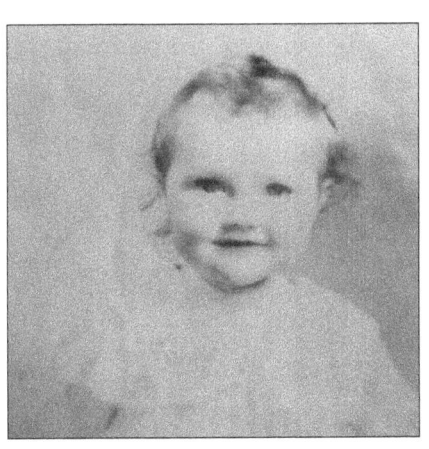

Once upon a time, a child, whose name was Mary, was born in Providence, Rhode Island, the youngest of five children. Her mother

Mary Croft

was thirty-seven and her father was forty-seven at the time of her birth, classifying her as a big surprise to the family.

Her brother, Thomas, made no bones about the fact that he adored her. He nicknamed her "Sugar" and when she was four years old he bought her a beautiful dark red tricycle with a bell on the right handle bar. She was thrilled as he watched her peddle for the very first time. Thomas was the little girl's idol. He was a great baseball player and she remembers admiring the trophies he won for his sportsmanship. She enjoyed his kind disposition and his ability to make her feel special, and, during World War II, she worried about him day and night until he returned home safely from Europe.

Letters to Barbara

They continued to share a loving relationship with each other for years to come, and he was the first person she called with questions about the past. His sharp memory for details and facts earned him the title of "family historian." When he died, the little girl, then an adult, wondered who would take his place in her life; but, of course, she quickly realized with great sadness that there would never be another Thomas.

Her other brother, James, was very quiet. On occasion, he would invite her, sometimes including one of her friends, to go to Waterman Lake with him. Quite exciting! He would rent a boat and paddle it out into the middle of the lake. Without saying more than a few words, "Wait for me in the boat," he would dive into the deep water and take a swim. Although she was scared, the little girl admired him for his bravery and never breathed a word to her parents about waiting alone in that boat. She feared they wouldn't let her go again and she loved the adventure. James' trophies were for his great agility and endurance when it came to running track in high school and college. Although he aspired to becoming a doctor, he found his way into the entertainment field after college. He formed a band, became a singer in local nightclubs, and eventually became manager of the Waterbury Elks Club where he continued to use his entertainment skills by hosting parties at which he frequently shared his gift of voice. He was the family radical, always doing the unusual. When he died, the little girl, then an adult, realized that there would never be another trip to Connecticut to visit James and his wife on their boat, Star IV.

Letters to Barbara

Dorothy was like a mother to her younger sister. Being fifteen years old when the child was born, she assumed a maternal role with her and was quite influential in her upbringing. She insisted that the child use proper enunciation when she spoke, reminding her to ask for "something" rather than "somethin." She also taught her to use perfect manners when answering the telephone. "Who's calling, please?" "Just a minute, please." Dorothy was a photographer by profession, which explains the many photos of the little girl wearing the perfectly-matching clothes that her sister chose for her. She was also a perfectionist in every way, and the child looked up to her for it. Although they were very different in personality and temperament, they had an admiration for each other which grew stronger with time and which developed into a life-long bond. When Dorothy died, the little girl, then an adult, felt as if she was losing her mother again. She then understood what Dorothy had told her many times, "I was your second mother."

Then, there was Barbara. Barbara was one of those special people, the type that everyone loves, the type that stands out, who always wears a smile, is fun-loving and makes you laugh. Her remarkable personality made it difficult for anyone to measure up to her. To the young child, Barbara was the physical image of Snow White. She had pale white skin, hazel eyes, and black hair that framed her beautiful face and then came to rest on her shoulders. The sisters loved each other very much. Barbara was, kind, generous, and self-sacrificing in all her relationships. You couldn't help but to love her. She was the big sister that anyone would be happy to have, the big sister that was always there, and the big sister that the child thought would be there for her for the rest of their lives. Unfortunately, unlike other

Letters to Barbara

fairy tales, this one did not end happily. On Mother's Day, 1946, Barbara died at age fifteen, leaving the small child behind, filled with grief that she could not understand. Grief that would travel with her every step of her way, grief that would depress her and stifle her journey because it would never be expressed and would never be shared with anyone for years to come. The little girl wondered what would become of her without her big sister and friend. She was terrified!

Mary Croft

But this is not the final chapter of the story, because years later Mary would be challenged to grieve that loss and to free herself from the bondage it created. With the help of God and a wonderful mentor, she would find herself living her journey one day at a time.

Learning how to grieve has transformed my life. It has taught me that each day is a gift and that each loss is an opportunity to grow. It is apparent to me that many of life's lessons have been learned on the tail of tragedy. Loss continues to be a part of my life, but it no longer controls my life.

In my youth, I believed that life could be wonderful but I wasn't really happy. It took three major depressions before I was introduced to a twelve-step program which would put me on the path to a better life, and it took the trauma of a divorce within my family to lead me to the place where I would learn that grieving is a process, a process that is absolutely necessary for me to live a healthy lifestyle.

The theme that runs through my life seems to be my need to fix every problem because in some way I feel responsible for it. My nagging feelings of guilt drive me to think I have to do something about everything, I never feel as if I have done enough, and I unconsciously put my focus on the happiness of others rather than on my own inner peace. Unfortunately unresolved losses and grief can do that to a person. It didn't help that, within me, the grief over my sister's death was living a silent life of its own; it helped even less that I had no idea that losing a sibling through death could cause survival guilt, the same type of guilt that the survivors of the Holocaust experienced. I was too young to know that loss and grief were becoming my driving forces. Years later, I would become aware that I had spent a lifetime trying to make up for something that wasn't my fault by attempting to keep everyone happy. It appeared that my parents were very unhappy and I thought I was the only one around to fix that! I thought it was my job to make up for my sister's death and for the unhappiness they suffered as a result of it. What did I know? I was only eight years old and living in my wonder years.

I suffered a trauma when Barbara died, a trauma that changed my life as well as the dynamics of my entire family. Some of the guilt I felt resulted from my feeling responsible for her death. I was haunted by those times we played our favorite game of jumping on the beds and she ended up with pains in her stomach. I just couldn't tell my parents that it was my fault. What would they think of me if they knew? I kept it to myself and unconsciously spent the rest of my life punishing myself for what I thought I did to my parents and hating myself even more for not owning up to it. My unspoken guilt would not only reside in my unconscious mind but would implant itself in my soul and rob me of so much joy.

Becoming an aunt at the early age of eight brought an element of joy into my life that was indescribable. Having older siblings paved the way for one birth after the other, and I quickly became surrounded by nieces and nephews. The enjoyment of spending time with them provided me with the distraction I needed to continue enjoying my childhood to some degree. I transitioned from treating my dolls like real people to treating my nieces and nephews like they were my own. There are no words to describe how much their love meant to me, and I have no idea what would have happened to me without them. I was able to go on with life with some degree of pleasure; however, I continued to react with guilt to just about everything that happened, guilt that wasn't clear to me at the time.

I recall feeling guilty, rather than proud, when I met with success in school. It was as if I didn't deserve the success because other students were not as lucky as I to have been an overachiever. I had been blessed with the skill of learning quickly and the determination to work hard, and I was raised by parents who valued intelligence. I had no idea I was carrying the baggage of survival guilt and that it was depriving me of enjoying what I deserved. What a terrible burden to carry, especially for a child. Spending a lifetime atoning for a crime I never committed became the real tragedy.

It didn't help that my parents' relationship changed drastically after my sister died. They either argued or employed the silent treatment. Honestly, I'm not sure which was worse. Although the arguing drove me crazy and made me feel fearful and helpless, the tension when they were silent with each other could be cut with a knife and it made me feel anxious. To this day, in all my relationships, the most powerful weapon to be used against me is emotional withdrawal in the form of silence. It's too reminiscent of the past. Anyone who knows me well knows that I need to express myself, I need to process situations, I need to talk about them! If only I had known that when Barbara died! Life could have been different for me. Perhaps, if my parents knew the importance of communicating their grief, they, too, could have avoided the conflict of acting out their feelings. Had we shared our grief, life could have been better for all of us.

Years after my sister's death, I heard something that described the unhappiness I felt as a child who lived in a household with parents who did not talk about things, who did not grieve. I was attending a conference and the keynote speaker said that the only thing children really want is for things to be "okay in the castle." How simple! Looking back I can understand why I felt the way I did. Things were not okay in my castle and I felt guilty because there didn't seem to be anything I could do to change that. If only I had known it wasn't my fault, if only I had known that it wasn't my job to make it okay in the castle, if only we had cried and grieved together. I just wanted all of us to be happy. Was that too much to expect?

Being the youngest in the family had its benefits, but it also had its negative effects. I felt inadequate, cute but inadequate. I was younger than the others, I was smaller than them, and I had less experience with life. If only once, somebody would seek my advice or ask for my opinion. But that's not the way it happened in our family. I tried to change that when I raised my youngest child, but I won't know the results of my efforts until she writes a book about her life.

At the time of my sister's death, the other siblings had moved on to college and/or marriage. In other words, they got on with their lives like most people do. Due to my feelings of guilt, I got on with the business of living for others rather than myself. I suddenly found myself alone in a castle where things weren't okay. Since nobody else was there, I assumed total responsibility for my parents' happiness. After all, if I wanted to be happy I would have to see to it that they were happy too. Isn't that what any eight-year-old child would do? Probably not, but with my temperament and motivated by the survival guilt I felt at the time, I unconsciously assumed the job of taking care of their problems and attempting to make things right. I worked very hard at it but, of course, nothing changed. Although we didn't talk about her, I knew they missed Barbara so I tried to make it up to them by becoming like her. I plodded along trying to do everything right, trying to be like my sister, trying to make up to them for their loss by imitating her ways. It wasn't that they expected this of me—it was just something I expected of myself—and at the time it seemed like the right thing to do. It's a reality check for me to look at pictures of myself back then. I appear so young and innocent, not at all capable of the responsibility I assumed.

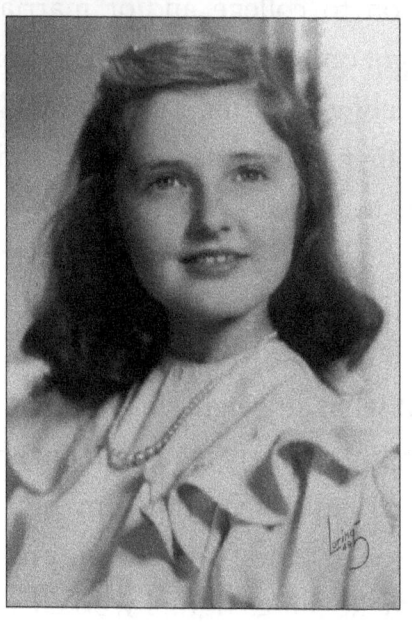

By nature I was a quiet child. I didn't make a lot of noise, I didn't ask a lot of questions, and I kept everything inside. Invisible seems to be a fitting term to describe myself at that age. Years later I learned that people are as sick as the secrets they keep, but who could I tell that I felt responsible for my sister's death and that

Letters to Barbara

I carried tremendous guilt for being the child who survived. And so my grief led me to a path of service to others at the expense of my own personal happiness. Without the knowledge of the grieving process, we tend to assume roles, expected or unexpected of ourselves, in order to relieve the anxiety created by the loss. We do what we think we should do rather than doing what we could do. And when you are compliant, this theory works for you, because it earns you the approval of others.

Years later, my mother told me that she regretted not getting help for me at the time of my sister's death, but I told her I understood. In 1946 people didn't have the luxury of mental health centers and support groups. My mother was a very perceptive woman, in spite of her age, and she was right about my need to talk about my trauma when my sister died. I believe that the real trauma was not only the incident that took place but the process that followed. Not getting it outside of myself did the real damage. I agreed with my mother that crying and talking about our grief would have been healthy for all of us, but I assured her that I understood she had done her best at the time.

Introspection has led me to realize that my temperament put me at risk for the path I followed after my first major loss. I was a sensitive child who found it difficult to make my needs known, and I can recall my struggle with separation problems at a very early age. My first experience with separation happened on the one and only day I attended kindergarten. I was only a little more than four at the time. It was a painful experience for me. I was fearful and shy and possibly a bit too young for school. There were so many butterflies flitting around in my stomach that day that I could barely eat my breakfast, the traditional "healthy" breakfast of bacon, eggs, and toast my mother cooked for us each and every morning. I was so excited about kindergarten that I ran ahead of my mother to the neighborhood school which was less than a block away. Ironically, I couldn't wait to get there! I was sporting a pretty new dress and my curls were tied up on the sides with ribbons. My mother was very proud of my banana curls since everyone who ever met me took notice of them and never failed to compliment her for them. She loved it!

The trouble started soon after we entered the school. There were very interesting things to see and the toys looked like fun but the kindergarten room was enormous and my best friend left me to play with the rest of the boy students. While the teachers were busy with the red tape of registering other students, my mother decided to leave without giving me warning. As I watched her body move as if in slow motion toward the exit door, I stood paralyzed, speechless, and afraid.

I felt all alone and I began to cry. Why didn't I call out to her? Why didn't I beg her to come back and sit with me until I found a friend? That's what most children would do, but it wasn't my nature; I was that timid four-and-a-half-year-old who kept her feelings inside and I remained paralyzed by the situation.

Mary Croft

I wish I could say that a wonderfully sensitive woman who was sitting nearby with her own child took my hand and comforted me, but unfortunately I can't! Instead I was faced with a cold, cruel, and insensitive person who witnessed my distress and who smirked at me with a grin on her face. She did not stop at that. As she smiled at me with disapproval, she proceeded to rub her index fingers together and gave me the "shame, shame" sign. Naturally, I cried even more because I felt embarrassed. I was trapped! I was four-and-a-half years old, I was attached to my mother, and I was left alone in a room full of strangers. "Aha, I'll escape," I thought. But the huge brass handle on that enormous solid oak door was just too much for me. I could barely reach it, never mind open it. Someone noticed my efforts and came to stop me. It felt like forever, but finally dismissal time arrived. As the students left the building, there was one small fearful child among them who vowed she would never go back. She would not feel good about it, but she would be too afraid to show up there again. She would feel trapped and she would experience that awful feeling that she felt whenever she was separated from her family, especially her mother. She would not explain her feelings to anyone because in her young

Letters to Barbara

mind there would be no labels for them. She would wonder every day what the other children were doing while she stayed at home, and she would be lonely because the neighborhood was quiet and there was nobody to play with her, but she would never take the chance of going back there to face that fear again. She would never risk being held hostage in that big room behind that large oak door with the big brass doorknob. Oh no, that would never happen no matter how lonely she felt! And when she saw the children carrying drawings and papers home to their parents, that little girl felt so inadequate because she was unable to do that. She would feel shame and guilt, and sadly nobody would know because she would not talk about it to anyone. She wouldn't know how to express herself. Looking back on that first and last day of kindergarten makes me realize that I was prone by my temperament to keep my emotions inside and so I assume some ownership for my inability to express my grief in the past.

My first depression came at the age of fourteen. It didn't last very long. I took the little pills that the family physician prescribed and in a few months I was back to normal; however, my grades suffered because I could

Mary Croft

not concentrate and I became one of those average students, no longer at the top of the class. I perceived myself as a disappointment to my parents. My mother especially prided herself in the fact that throughout elementary school I had been a straight "A" student which, by the way, had earned me a full scholarship to a Catholic high school. I felt so inadequate because here I was thinking it was my job to keep my parents happy and instead I was becoming, by my standards, a failure in school. My self-esteem went down the tubes when I needed it most. Eventually, I accepted my average-student title and in four years I graduated from high

Letters to Barbara

school. I was offered a well-paying job as a medical secretary for a highly respected orthopedic surgeon on the East Side of Providence.

As fate would have it, my life moved on. On Christmas Eve, 1958, I became engaged to my soulmate, that tall dark handsome guy by the name of John Howard Croft, and we began planning our wedding for July 4th, 1959, Independence Day!!

Now remember that gnawing feeling I mentioned about having to keep my parents happy? Well, needless to say, I felt sure that I was about to abandon them by leaving home to get married. Sensing this, the fear and guilt returned in such great proportions that I became triggered into another major depression. This time, I received my help from a very wise doctor who practiced neurology and psychiatry. He came with great credentials and a history of having successfully treated a young member of our family for a rare disorder of the nervous system known as St. Vitus Dance. It was necessary, at the time, to refer to this wonderful doctor as a neurologist. We could never mention the psychiatry part of his practice because my mother had a problem with that. It seems that I saw him only several times, but his caring nature and the pills he prescribed did the trick and I was well on my way to the "big day." As I mentioned, he was a very wise doctor and with his help I was able to enjoy the excitement surrounding my wedding plans. It was a great distraction from the baggage of grief I unconsciously carried.

And so, I temporarily recovered from another depression, and again, the healing came from the outside. No talking about my emotions, no therapy, no processing. It was the 1950's and that wasn't popular yet. But the treatment brought a certain degree of healing, enough to make it possible to plan my wedding and to hope for the life in which I expected to live happily ever after in that castle I mentioned. Unfortunately, I remained oblivious to the grief that was storing up inside

Letters to Barbara

of me. The guilt of abandoning my parents and the loss of the only place I had ever called home weighed heavily on my spirit, but I managed to rise above my depression and vowed to create my own castle, the one in which everything would be okay.

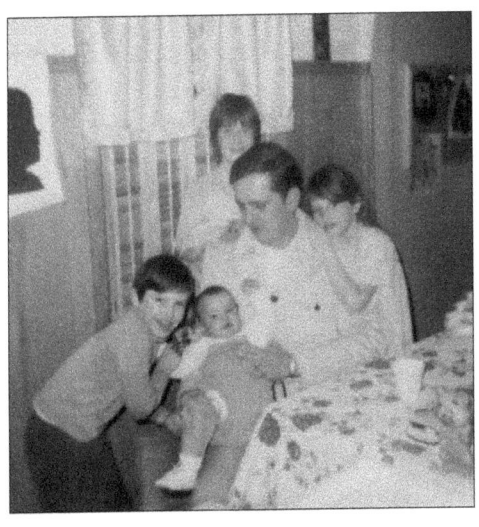

I loved being a housewife and a stay-at-home mother; it was more fun than playing house as a child. I had a real house, a real husband and four precious children, not dolls but real little people. Although I continued to struggle with depression and anxiety from time to time, I did everything possible to make things okay in the castle. I was determined that my children would be reared in happy surroundings, and, surprisingly, I taught them to freely express themselves. One thing of which I was certain, I didn't want my children to develop the same destructive pattern of stifling themselves by holding their emotions inside. That was one mistake I would try not to repeat, one more step I would take toward making it okay in the castle for my children.

Life continued to provide losses and, like everyone else, I had many encounters with grief. I had feelings of sadness, despair, loneliness, disappointment, and guilt; but it didn't occur to me that I could label those feelings or put them into perspective by sharing them because I didn't have the awareness or the skill.

Letters to Barbara

Today, my life is an adventure. I know that grief is a very natural phenomenon and I am able to identify my feelings of loss, to accept loss for what it is, and to take the necessary action, which is the grieving process, to free myself from the bondage it can create.

The following chapters will explore my various encounters with grief, my futile efforts to run away from the feelings that accompany grief, and the freedom I have attained by using the grieving process. I invite all who read *Letters to Barbara* to create your own adventurous journey. Educate yourself about loss, recognize grief and its effects on your life, and move on by developing a formula of grieving that will make your life the beautiful adventure story it was intended to be.

The Journey Begins

> "Dear Barbara,
>
> Where do I begin? It is so many years ago since you left and so much has happened. Although I missed you back then, I miss you in a different way now, a way that is difficult to describe. I try to imagine what our relationship would be like and how it would be to have you as my friend. I fantasized over the years and thought about how different my life would have been if you were here for me. Right now, as I wander through a very dark tunnel, I can only hope that writing letters to you will make a difference in my life...."

Letters to Barbara

My first major loss traumatized me because I was only eight years old when it happened. Being an exceptionally quiet child and coming from a family that didn't discuss feelings, the opportunity to grieve my sister's death was not presented to me. I felt sad after the death of my fifteen-year-old sister but above all I felt lonely and guilty. I realized many years later that it's perfectly normal to feel loneliness and guilt after a loss. It's sort of like a package deal: loss, loneliness, and guilt equal grief. There was no healing for me at the time and it remained inside of me for many years. It's not that I intentionally turned my back on my grief, but my family, which was my only social network at the time, didn't discuss it. As a matter of fact, on the day following Barbara's death, as my mother got me ready for school, her last words to me were, "If anyone mentions Barbara, tell them your mother said not to talk about it." Of course, people asked questions but all I could do was cry. My wonderful third-grade teacher, Sister Marion, took me into another room where she gave me her white linen handkerchief and helped me to wipe my tears. I felt so confused. Consequently, when I suffered other losses in my life I reacted much like an eight-year-old; I would become filled with fear and anxiety because

Mary Croft

I did not understand my emotions, and I would keep my feelings inside not sharing them with anyone.

Time passed and a divorce in my immediate family triggered me into a state of grief. The divorce, although it wasn't mine, was tragic for me, so tragic that it forced me to seek help. It was at that point that I was introduced to the process of grieving. I've come to view the process as an art, one which develops and improves with time, and I have since committed myself to the daily routine of recognizing and accepting the losses that enter my life and of grieving them as they occur.

At the time of the divorce, my life seemed to turn upside down. I began wondering about everything and anything that had provided me with meaning in life, and I questioned my purpose for being here on this wonderful Earth. I felt very alone. Although there were other people in my home during my long dark sleepless nights, all comfortably snoozing in their warm beds, I might as well have been at the bottom of the sea where the only sign of life to encounter is the light of the luminescent fish who live there. I felt completely alone in my misery.

Over and over, I asked myself why this was happening. I felt so threatened by it, I felt as if my entire world was falling apart. And it was! It was difficult to imagine life any other way than the way it had been before this divorce. At times it felt surreal, as if it wasn't happening at all; but then the phone would ring or the smoke alarm would go off because the potatoes were burning, and the painful reality would strike again! My entire physical, mental, and spiritual being wanted to believe that the event was not happening, but denial and deception had never been luxuries in my life, and so I was forced to plod through the doom of my grief.

Nothing seemed to ease my pain or provide relief for me. I was like a little child, lost in a forest from which there was no escape. I actually thought of death as an escape from the pain. How tragic for me to entertain such thoughts, the person who loved life. A person who, before this happened, could sit by the ocean and be healed by the overpowering smell of the salty fresh air and by the unending sound of the waves breaking around me in perfect cadence. But I could find no relief from my pain this time around.

The gift of desperation led me to reach out for help. I contacted a counselor with whom I was familiar. She is a woman of deep compassion and sensitivity, someone whose ability to listen without judging is unique. She is a gifted woman who brings these qualities and more into the counseling relationship, a rare individual who is willing to go beyond the call of duty to provide nurturance as well as knowledge to her clients. I don't know how she manages it, but she never watches the clock. She makes her clients feel as if she is on their time, not hers, a rarity in the field of mental health. Because I was feeling so vulnerable at the time, I needed to be in a safe place, and her office became my haven. Thank you, Cheryl, from the bottom of my heart.

She asked me if I had ever done "grief work" and, of course, I hadn't. Remember now, I came from an Irish/Scotch Catholic family whose culture was of a private nature. As for feelings and situations, you were told not to "let on" to anybody about anything. It wasn't part of the family system to talk about feelings. Cheryl encouraged me to start a journal, one in which I would write letters to my sister, Barbara. I made no connection between this childhood tragedy of the past and my reaction to the recent divorce, but I trusted her judgement and knew that the journal could not do me any harm. And so the process began.

My lifetime thirst for learning had never been quenched by time or age and my search for truth had al-

Letters to Barbara

ways taken precedence in my life. I lived with the firm belief that truth and freedom were one. And so, in my quest to understand my dilemma and to heal myself, I began to journal to my sister with the hope that I would find an answer to the sadness and grief that had permeated my entire life. I called the journal "Letters to Barbara."

When my sister died many years before the divorce, I had no idea that it was natural to feel lonely and guilty as a result of grief; so what did I do with those emotions? Feeling ashamed of them, I buried them. I blamed myself for that terrible tragedy on Mother's Day, 1946. I was absolutely certain that her appendix had burst because of one of those times when we jumped on our beds and tickled each other until we fell on the floor. I was driven by the guilt I felt; but instead of processing it, I lived my life trying to make up for it. I wondered, too, why she had died and I continued living. I was traumatized by survival guilt. Having never dealt with this survival guilt, I began to find ways of blaming myself for the divorce that was taking place.

The letters to my sister took me back to my younger years, and my conversations with Barbara surprised me. I began to identify the roots to some of my personality traits: people pleasing, feeling unworthy, blaming and punishing myself, etc. I began to realize that there was so much living that I could have done if only I had been able to grieve. Instead, I had accumulated a volume of unresolved losses.

And so, I committed myself to this task called "the grieving process" and thus began the wonderful journey into the heart and soul of myself, the self into which I was born, the self I was meant to be, the self that was waiting to be free. I continued to journal daily and to discuss my growing awareness with Cheryl. As I said, her office was my haven at that very vulnerable time. It was amazing how many incidents had triggered my feelings of loss and guilt over the years. Eventually, I came to accept that grief is like hunger, it occurs daily, and that grieving is like food, it pacifies!

I can't say it was a painless project but certainly I can say that it opened up another chapter of my life that had been stored away in the attic of my mind, a chapter that was screaming out to be lived. As I paid attention to the letters I was writing to my sister, I began to understand the connection between her death and the recent divorce. Similarly, when my sister died a sudden death many years before the divorce, I was unexpectedly thrown into a world I was unable to understand. She was gone, I was abandoned, and everything changed for me. Life lost its color, the world became grey, and I was alone with the pain. This was the connection. The loss was different but the emotional experience was the same. I was repeating the pattern that was woven so many years previously. I was stuck in my grief, I was reacting to it rather than working through it. I had heard that grief was cumulative and that each loss triggers previous losses; but, until that epiphany, I had not comprehended the true meaning of those facts.

Eventually, I came to accept the divorce. I have learned to accept it and to live in spite of it. It forced me to learn how to grieve, not to forget but to grieve, to enter into a process without getting stuck in a situation. At times, I am still that lost child in a dark forest, but I no longer feel alone and helpless because I now have a formula to grieve. I've learned that there are tools to guide me from the darkness of the forest into the brightness of the colorful field. There is now a path that guides me to the destination of hope and contentment. It is a process that has become part of me and which takes its place at the top of my priority list.

Mary Croft

My greatest awareness along the way has been that, as humans, we perpetually experience losses; and whether they are major or minor losses, they affect us. These losses will cause us grief and the impact can be devastating; but we have the opportunity to work our way through to the light at the end of the tunnel by refusing to allow our grief to victimize us. There is a way! It's necessary to open your mind to the possibility that everyday losses are affecting you. You need to identify them, accept that they cause you grief, and move on by grieving them as they occur. Know that they will continue to haunt you if you fail to greet them!

What's It All About

As I said, when my sister died, I had no concept of loss, I had no idea of the impact it was having on me, and I certainly had not acquired any skills to deal with the situation. I believed my emotions at the time, I buried them deeply, and I was driven by them. Again, what did I know at the age of eight? Absolutely nothing! I barely knew about life and there I was facing death. I had no idea that, although my sister had died, my grief would continue to live and to quietly haunt me, determining my direction as I journeyed through life.

Loss is inevitable. It happens to us in different ways every day. True that it's painful, but it must be embraced because, without connecting to it, it causes a state of grief that doesn't go away. The path to healing is to work through it by finding a way to process it. It will not heal itself and it will not disappear. It's very important to make a connection between the losses you encounter daily and the grief you feel as a result. Before I made this connection, I was a stranger to myself. I was stuck between the person I thought I should be and the person I wanted to be. And I was resentful that my life had gone in that direction.

Recognizing our daily losses is vital to a healthy lifestyle. When someone dies, the loss is obvious because, suddenly, something in the present becomes a thing of the past. Others express their sympathy by engaging in conversations with us about the person. We are inclined to reminisce and to share memories of them with others. But when losses occur that have nothing to do with death, very often they go unrecognized. Simple change brings about feelings of loss. Think of all the changes, major and minor, that go on from day to day. We may not connect them to feelings of grief; therefore, we may not give them the attention they deserve. We end up with a pile of unfinished business that gets bur-

Letters to Barbara

ied alive. We accumulate a storage bin of negative emotions which get triggered by other losses and cause more unresolved grief. Fortunately, we are not faced with death every day but we will undoubtedly encounter losses.

Loss is a personal matter. Not all individuals experience it for the same reasons. Our reactions to situations might be different, but the result is always the same—it causes grief. By grief, I mean a feeling of stress, unease, sadness, confusion, and the list goes on to include any negative emotion you can imagine; but the final analysis is that grief makes you feel unhealthy. The good news is that you can do something about it. Sometimes, just knowing it's there helps me to understand my grief and to accept it as a natural reaction to my situation. There may not be anything I can do about it, but I can simply recognize it and understand it.

Looking back, there were so many times when I didn't feel well and had no idea why. I remember as a child feeling so sad when a friend moved away, never to be heard from again. I wondered what happened to her for years. And then there was the time when a friend got very sick and was taken to the hospital. Until she returned home, I thought I'd never see her again. When my brothers were drafted into the service during wartime, I felt a deep dark hole inside of me, a hole which nothing could fill. I remember losing my first teeth. Although I waited anxiously for the coins from the tooth fairy, I hated the thought of losing something that was so much a part of me! Surrendering my dolls to younger relatives, when everyone else thought I was too old for them, was tragic for me. They were my babies. I still remember their names. When I moved on to high school and had to travel out of my familiar surroundings, I was extremely uncomfortable, just as I was whenever I tried to stay away from home for a sleepover. It was a mountain to climb when I moved away from my parents to start my own home.

Changes caused by separation can cause loss. After the birth of each child, I suffered from post-partum blues. It puzzled me because one of my very first memories was an intense longing to have children. In retrospect, I understand it now. It was loss that created the grief I felt back then. You see, I never felt better than when I was pregnant. Knowing I had life growing inside of me, nurturing that life by eating well and following doctor's orders, feeling the movement of the baby inside my body created a feeling of emotional wellness

Letters to Barbara

in me that could not compare to anything else. Being on an emotional high every day, it's not any wonder that I was suffering from physical separation from my babies after their births. When I began to educate myself about the effects of loss, I realized that the sadness and depression I felt after I gave birth was the result of no longer carrying that child inside of me, the loss of the physical closeness that only pregnancy can offer. Because I didn't talk about it with anyone, it did not get processed. Fortunately, the busy-ness of having a newborn provided the distraction I needed to move on; however, it simply added to the accumulation of unresolved losses that haunted me.

Mary Croft

I can remember feeling sad when my children went back to school every September after a great summer of fun. I loved the time I spent with them. I enjoyed taking them on trips, going to the park, the zoo. They were my treasures and their fun was my enjoyment. At that time, I had no idea that my sadness was due to feelings of grief. As I said, some losses are difficult to recognize.

Many years ago, my sister-in-law, Jackie, suffered a gum disease as the result of a pregnancy. It was necessary for her to have her teeth extracted and to wear dentures. I noticed that she seemed very affected by the situation. She wasn't herself. I didn't understand it at the time, but looking back I realize that she suffered deep grief about losing the beautiful teeth she once had. Although she continued to exhibit her magnetic personality and undeniable beauty, she never truly smiled in the same way after that loss. It wasn't until after I was introduced to the grieving process and I unexpectedly lost a tooth in the middle of a Christmas Eve celebration that I realized the depth of Jackie's loss. I regret that I missed the opportunity to offer her the support she so deserved, but, at the time, I didn't hear the heart that grieved. May you rest in peace, my beautiful friend.

For ten years, I worked as a Substance Abuse Counselor at an in-patient facility. By the time a person finds themselves in a treatment program, addiction has led them to believe that it is their best friend and they are dependent on the lifestyle that accompanies the addiction. Often the clients would relapse after discharge and return for another round of treatment. It was apparent that most of the clients who chronically relapsed had not grieved the lifestyle that had accompanied their drinking days. They had, as we hear often, tried to put the cart before the horse. They were attempting to abstain from the alcohol or other drugs without grieving the people, places, and things that accompanied it, without making the necessary adjustments. They failed to recognize the loss of their previous identity as a user; and without working through the excruciating painful process of that sadness, they were unable to maintain their sobriety. It's said that the degree of grief you feel is closely related to the degree of dependence you have toward the loss. Makes sense to me that the unrecognized and unprocessed grief associated with early-stage sobriety could be a major stumbling block for anyone trying to live the straight life. The entire package needs to be identified and grieved.

It might seem that losing a job would be a minor loss; but, when you have a deep attachment to what you are doing and to the people involved, it can be devastating. I once left a job that I loved because of a values conflict with a co-worker. We worked very closely together in an educational program for troubled youth. After giving it about a year with this person, it was pointed out to me that the job as I had known it no longer existed. We had very different values and goals which interfered with our ability to productively work together. Both the administrators and the students wanted me to stay, but in spite of my love for the job I chose to make a healthy decision and I left. The pain I suffered from that loss was tremendous, and it took action on my part to heal from it. Although I enjoyed the new job, thoughts of my "old life" kept haunting me; but if I was not tuned in to the grief I was feeling, I would not have understood my distress. I grew so much from that experience because I recognized it, I accepted it as a loss, and I journeyed myself through the long dark tunnel it created.

Years ago, after being introduced to a 12-step program, I began my journey of self-inventory, of introspection, of spiritual growth. The most important part of that program was to build on my strengths while trying to weed out my defects of character at the same time. I was quick to recognize my faults and to admit to them, but when it came to letting go of them it was difficult for me because they were such a part of who I was at the time. I remember talking endlessly about them to other members of my group and wondering why it was so difficult for me. I realize now that change, whether it's negative or positive, is a loss that causes a sadness which must be grieved.

Mary Croft

Aging creates a unique set of losses with which to deal, and the losses are universal to all of us regardless of our differences. Loss of partners, parents, siblings accompanied by the personal losses of mobility, strength, vision, hearing, status, importance, health, etc., affects all of us in some way, and to deny this loss can isolate us from ourselves and those we love by keeping us stuck in our grief. Aging brings about so many daily losses that an entire book could be devoted to it, but for now I want to state that much of my present grief is the result of the aging process. Loss is inescapable, but recognizing it, accepting it, and grieving it is possible.

Before *Letters to Barbara* I had no understanding of the connection of my daily losses to my feelings of grief. I found myself living in a state of perpetual anxiety, uncomfortable in my own skin, always doubting myself, and not knowing the reason. Always feeling incomplete, like something was missing, and trying to compensate by filling my life with busyness. I knew nothing about grief except that it was painful, and I made every attempt to run away from it. But the only thing I got away from was myself! The healing didn't take place and the wounds didn't heal from the inside out; emotions were buried alive and poisoned my spirit. Presently I believe that I am defined by my grief and I need to become a friend to myself by actively participating in it. It's a priority now to clear my mind as well as my house daily. That pile of negative emotions caused by losses will do me more harm than the dust bunnies under the furniture.

Grief and grieving are companions; however, they are not the same. They are partners but each possesses its own characteristics. Grief is a passive condition, one that happens to us, but grieving is an active process, something we do. Grief is a state of mind, body, and spirit during which we feel distress. It manifests itself in feelings of loneliness, guilt, anger, frustration, just to name a few. It shows up without invitation and is rarely considered a welcomed caller. Sometimes we are prepared for its visit but most times it presents itself abruptly and comes without warning. I have yet to meet anybody who consciously invites grief, nor do I know of anybody who welcomes it. While grief happens "to" us, grieving happens "because" of us. My unresolved grief disguised itself as a depression which promised to fade away with time, distraction, and medical attention. However, it never kept its promise!

Mary Croft

Grieving does not come to us, we must pursue it. It requires a conscious effort and a personal commitment from us to actively engage in its process. It is a task and requires certain skills, skills that are very different for each individual. It's like buying a pair of shoes—you need to find the right fit. I have found that communicating my feelings to selected individuals and writing about situations in the form of letters works best for me, but there are other activities that serve people as well. It's important to tap into your creativity in order to develop the style that works best for you. Everyone is unique, so everyone has preferences when it comes to the grieving process.

Grieving does not make us forget, it simply helps us to remember the loss with less pain. Just recently, while driving my car, I was reminded of the day my daughter died. You might wonder why the memory surfaced while driving on a busy highway, but it was triggered by my senses. The atmosphere of the day was similar to that tragic day. It was grey and cloudy outside and it was about five o'clock in the afternoon, the same time of day that I received the tragic news. It was as if a scar had opened up and I could feel the impact of the pain I felt that September day in 2006. Being behind the wheel of my car, I was unable to take out a pen and write or to call a friend and talk; but I began to verbalize my feelings by speaking them aloud as I cried my tears of sorrow. Yes, I gave myself permission to remember my loss, knowing that it can surface at any time without warning, but I was remembering it with a sense of understanding. It comforted me to know that I had embraced the loss without getting stuck in the grief. By crying and verbalizing, I was putting my grief outside of myself rather than burying it inside.

Grieving has allowed me to continue living in spite of my losses and it has invited me to do pleasurable things even when I have no desire to do so. I equate it with putting one foot in front of the other when I'd rather stand still. Living is about being and doing, so on we must go.

While grief is a set of symptoms, grieving is a set of tasks. Grief is binding and keeps us in a state of physical, mental, and spiritual distress. Grieving, however, is freeing and allows us to live in spite of our losses. It invites us to heal from the inside out so that we may find peace and even happiness in our life after loss. Grieving lightens the burden by getting the grief into the open, by not allowing it to accumulate and become an unnecessary weight to be carried.

Grief will be part of our lives forever because we will always experience losses. We will say farewell to family members, pets, jobs, friends, and all sorts of things, and because of our immortality we will watch ourselves and others age. Nothing is permanent, life is about change, so there will be losses on a daily basis. Our goal is to identify the loss, to accept it, and to experience healing by using the grieving process.

We have the privilege to emerge from the solitude of our losses into a world of no limitations, an adventurous journey. We can gift ourselves with a second chance to live life from the inside out and to be free to sing and dance to our own personal rhythms. We can embrace our grief by connecting it to the losses we encounter in our daily living, and we can process our grief by engaging in it and finding ways to get it outside of ourselves. Since I was introduced to the process of grieving, I have developed the awareness that most of my stress is due to some feeling of loss, some type of change in myself or the world around me, some type of uncertainty. That loss does not go away, it simply takes on a life of its own. I now have the choice to grieve or not to grieve.

Letters to Barbara invites you to find your way out of your fairy tale and into your adventure story by recognizing, accepting, and grieving your losses in your own unique way. Happy journey!

Memories of My Grandmother

My maternal grandmother, Euphemia P. Hoag, died in 1960. When she died

Letters to Barbara

I had no idea that grieving was a process, and her death was my first major loss after the death of my sister. Having lived with our family for many years and being the only grandmother I knew, she had played a major role in my life. I remember feeling great compassion for her because she was financially poor and endured a great deal of hardship in her life. She also suffered from arthritis and was in pain most of the time.

My grandmother was born in Dundee, Scotland, in 1878. Her family came to the United States when she was ten years old. They lived in what was known as the Smith Hill section of Providence where she, her siblings, and parents all became citizens. At that time, immigrants who had the good fortune of establishing themselves in this country would open their homes to others from their native countries and help them to set up residency here. That's how it was for my grandfather, James Sharpe. His family had known my grandmother's family in Scotland and was aware that they had established citizenship in the United States; and so arrangements were made for him to travel here and to stay with them until he gained citizenship. He was fourteen years old at the time. He became what they referred to as a "boarder" in my grandmother's home, and so began the relationship between my mother's parents. Eventually, they married.

Letters to Barbara

James Sharpe worked for an exclusive restaurant and catering service on the East Side of Providence. My mother was proud to let us know that he was a talented baker who actually designed the desserts he made. One of her regrets was that she was unable to locate an old book containing pictures of the cookies he had designed. In those days, people seldom owned property; they rented tenements and shared attics to store their treasures. Items got moved around and their whereabouts forgotten; hence, the disappearance of the treasured cookie album!

When my grandfather died at the early age of twenty-four, my grandmother was left with two very young children, my mother and her brother, James. She did what most widowed women had to do in the late

Mary Croft

1800's and she remarried. She then had six more children, two of whom died in infancy, leaving my mother to be raised in a family of six.

Years later, her oldest son, James, died at the young age of thirty-one. All the more reason for me to pity my grandmother. It seems that her life was filled with tragedy, and the sadness she projected must have been from the weight of her grief.

As I watched her age, my compassion for her grew stronger. Knowing the hardship she endured and watching her in pain every day was very difficult for me; it made me want to help her but all I could do was to make her feel better by offering my love and attention when she needed it. My grandmother's death actually came as a relief to me because knowing she was no

Letters to Barbara

longer in pain brought me comfort. As I said, I knew nothing about grieving so I was bewildered by my reaction. Today I realize that some losses do bring relief depending on the circumstances. I wasn't privileged with that information in 1960.

There are some positive memories of my grandmother that I treasure. She was the most humble woman I ever met, not pretentious in any way. She drank her tea from the saucer, which is traditional for Scotch people, but she insisted the reason was that "it's cooler that way." I suppose she had a point, but I like to remember it as part of her Scottish culture. She loved homemade apple turnovers with her tea. She made it very clear to family and friends that the apple turnovers my mother baked were exclusively for her. We were welcome to the apple pie, but the turnovers had her name on them. With that said, nobody dared to smell them let alone eat them. If you wanted to tease my grandmother, just browse by the apple turnovers—it worked every time.

When she died in 1960, my first child was six months old. The timing of her death was fortunate for me, if there is such a thing, because having a new baby to love and nurture provided me with a great distraction from my grief. I can still remember the relief when I attended my grandmother's wake to see her free from pain and looking more peaceful than I had ever seen her. After her death, whenever I felt sad and lonely, I would revert to that peaceful expression on her face and I would feel a sense of comfort.

I realize now that I inadvertently grieved my grandmother's passing. We were temporarily living with my parents which gave me exposure to a great support system. It was a busy household with family and friends coming and going at a rapid pace. I invited myself into their conversations and reminisced about my grandmother which, by the way, is a great tool for grieving. It would be years later, after being introduced to the grieving process, that I would realize how important the tools of connecting and communicating are in the face of loss.

I'm certain that the balance of focusing my attention on my newborn daughter, of exposing myself to the conversations of friends and family, and of believing that my grandmother was finally at peace helped me to deal with her death at a time when I knew nothing about dealing with grief.

Tea and apple turnovers will forever trigger a memory of my dear grandmother.

Remembering My Father

My father, Thomas F. Mahar, was born in Providence, Rhode Island, in 1892, to Mary Cronin and John Mahar. He was the oldest of three sons, all of whom preceded him in death. We attributed his good health and longevity to the fact that he preferred walking to riding no matter what the distance. Anyone who walked with my father had to run to keep up with his pace.

I was told he was a devoted son. At the age of fourteen, he went to work, and with his very first paycheck, he bought his mother a beautiful crystal mug which is now considered a family heirloom. He was fond of the jewelry trade; however, back in the early 1900's most men, especially the Irish, worked on the railroad. And so it was, he got a job in the Charles Street station of the New York, New Haven, and Hartford Railroad, the

Letters to Barbara

location of which has since lent itself to the famous Interstate 95 in Providence. On Sundays, my mother would prepare a hot lunch for my father and Barbara and I would walk to the Charles Street Station to deliver it to him. My mother would neatly pack the lunch in a bowl, wrap the bowl in a towel to keep the food warm, and then place the bowl in a bag for easy carrying. This was many years before the invention of insulated lunch bags. Barbara, because she was older, had the job of carrying the lunch while I went along as company for her. My father never failed to warn us in his overprotective way, "When you cross the railroad bridge, don't look through the peep holes. You might get soot in your eyes." The temptation was so great and we loved seeing the trains moving along the tracks, so, of course, we peeked through every hole we could find on that bridge and never once got soot in our eyes. When we finally arrived at the station, my father would greet us with a big smile. His face was black with soot, and when he smiled his teeth glistened. The whites of his blue eyes stood out like cumulus clouds in the sky on a bright day. We loved my father and he loved us for sure. He was so proud of Barbara and me and so happy to show us off to his co-workers. I think he enjoyed that more than the lunch we delivered to him. Although, I must say my mother was an awesome cook!

Working on the railroad was a seven-day-a-week job including holidays. Each Christmas we would wait impatiently for him to come home from work to open his presents that were still under the tree. Not that he was going to be surprised! Barbara and I gave him the exact same thing each year, a shaving mug and a brush. He would arrive home about 3:30 PM, and we would plead with him to open the presents before he ate his Christmas dinner. We just couldn't wait. It didn't seem fair to me that he had to work on Christmas but it didn't seem to bother my father at all. He never complained, he had a strong work ethic which I admired about him.

The stories my father told us about his boyhood were great. One of my favorites is the winter tale of his skating on the pond in Providence with his friends. Without fail, someone would fall through the ice. They would build a fire and, while their clothes were drying over the heat, the potatoes would be baking in the ground. Listening to him was like being there. You could almost taste those potatoes and feel the warmth of the blazing fire.

Letters to Barbara

His summertime excursions to Oakland Beach in Warwick were just as interesting. On Sunday, he and his friends would walk from Providence to Warwick which took them about three hours. They would spend the entire day at Oakland Beach where they swam and then played around at the amusement park until it was time to start their three-hour journey home. It was his manner of telling the story that made it fascinating. I could feel his sense of enjoyment and comradery, and I could vividly imagine the fun he and his friends had experienced. Memories of my father would not be complete without mentioning that, in his twenty's, he was the proud manager of the Capitol AC's, a local baseball group in Providence, RI.

The Capital AC's, of Providence, pose after their championship game in 1912. My father, Thomas Mahar (third from the left in the front row), was their manager.
Mary Croft, Warwick

Mary Croft

These and many more of my father's stories are neatly bound in my mental notebook of "Good Memories and Funny Stories." They are often shared and never to be forgotten!

In my adulthood, Oakland Beach became one of my favorite spots, one of the places I would frequent, rain or shine, summer and winter. It became the place where I found my connection to God and the universe, a place where I would walk the shore and cry the tears that I had buried for years, tears that I felt ashamed to express. You might say that I did some of my grieving there without knowing it. Something about the sound and smell of the ocean and the feeling of the salt-air breeze on my face lifts my spirit no matter how low I feel. It's a place where I feel so connected to my father and the memories he shared about the location. I feel grateful that I inherited his love of the ocean and that I have the privilege of living in the Ocean State where I am surrounded by shoreline and where I can feed my soul without traveling far.

When they married in 1918, my father, Thomas Mahar, was twenty-seven and my mother, Agnes Sharpe, was seventeen. They made many happy memories raising five children together, but, after my sister's

Letters to Barbara

death, their relationship changed. My father would sit alone in the living room, crying until he sobbed. My mother and I would be at the opposite end of the house in the kitchen. I couldn't understand why they didn't connect with each other; it terrified me that they didn't. Although my mother didn't cry much, I knew her heart was broken and that she missed my sister as much as my father did, but she wasn't one to show her feelings. It wasn't her style. One day I noticed that Barbara's graduation picture was missing from its resting place on top of the upright piano in the living room. My mother said she had put it away because it made my father cry. Such a beautiful picture of my sister, looking like an angel in her white graduation dress with her wavy black hair framing her gorgeous snowy white face. Why would we hide such a treasure from view? Removing that picture made no sense to me, but I didn't feel as if I had the right to pass my opinion about it. It simply added to the loss I felt and reinforced the attitude that you don't talk about your feelings and that you remove any reminders of the loss. Although my mother believed she was doing a kind act on my father's behalf, I realize now that it was a missed opportunity for all of us as a family. We could have embraced each other, my mother and father and I, and we could have cried and reminisced about our love for Barbara. We could have grieved our tragic loss and possibly encountered some healing. Who knows, I might have admitted to my guilt feeling about being the one who survived. I might have gotten my parents' reassurance that I had the right to live and that my survival guilt was a normal reaction to my grief over the loss I had recently encountered.

Talking about it could have been a great opportunity for all of us, and I could have learned, at the young age of eight, that when there is loss there is grief, when there is grief there are tears, and that crying is part of the grieving process and creates healing. But I simply learned to bury my emotional pain. Unfortunately, my pain was buried alive!

My father and sister were close and did many things together; after she died I lived with the nagging feeling that I was all he had left in this world. I prided myself in my ability to understand him and to see him in his true light. As time went on, I developed a deeper closeness with my father. I felt like I understood him more than the other important people in his life. I think it was because I tried to make it up to him for the loss of my sister and also because we had much in common. We both loved animals and had a similar appreciation of nature.

Mary Croft

Every Spring, my father planted a garden of beautiful Marigolds in an area which bordered the cement steps that led from our backyard to the front of our house on Jenkins Street in Providence. Suddenly, without warning, those lovely buds would pop their pretty little heads out of the ground and in no time at all they would become a gorgeous mix of orange and yellow ballerinas dancing in the wind. I can't remember descending those steps without stopping to admire my father's ability to grow such a beautiful garden. The beauty and wonder of those flowers fascinated me as a child and they fascinate me now! I plant them in my vegetable garden each spring as a natural deterrent to the insects, and a pot of them takes residence on my father's grave on Father's Day each June. I regret not having asked him why, year after year, he planted only Marigolds when there were so many other types of flowers available to him. My imagination leads me to believe that he planted them in memory of his mother, my grandmother, whose name was Mary. I remain in awe of my father's dedication to the memory of my grandmother and to those velvety yellow and orange Marigolds that flaunted their pretty little faces every Spring and Summer.

Letters to Barbara

My father instilled in me an appreciation of nature. That appreciation has followed me through my life and has been a great friend to me especially in times of grief. Feeling at one with nature is a healing experience for me.

As my father aged, we actually spent more quality time together. My children loved him and were excited to have him visit especially when he slept over. He would spoil them with fast food, ice cream, and all the goodies that kids love. He always brought his bag of tools with him just in case there was something that needed fixing. One day he decided to build a shed in our backyard to store the kids' bikes and other toys. He elicited the help of my neighbor whom he knew personally for years. Before the project was finished, the neighbor invited my dad to lunch at a local bar. We laughed for years about the fact that we ended up with a crooked shed as a result of that lunch they shared, and we could only speculate about what they had to drink with their lunch that day! The shed was higher on one side than the other; however, we did have a shed. That was my father!

Although I was the youngest child, my dad became more dependent upon me as he aged. I had assumed responsibility for his happiness from the time of Barbara's death, and he trusted me and valued my opinions. He confided in me and sought my advice on just about everything. I drove him to doctor appointments and I advocated for him whenever necessary. I was there for him just as my sister would have been. Having lived my life feeling inadequate and unimportant, this role I assumed with my father was a great boost to my ego.

As our relationship grew closer over the years, our understanding of each other deepened as well. We had a mutual bond, and memories of my father are stored with a special fondness. I never tire of the memories my father created.

My father died suddenly at one of the most difficult times in my life. I was being treated for another depression. It is obvious to me that the chaos in my personal life, at that time, served as a great distraction from the grief I felt as the result of my father's death, a loss for which I was very ill-prepared. It didn't matter that he was eighty years old at the time; his unexpected death shocked me and exacerbated my depression and anxiety. It didn't help that, while facing this tragic loss, I had no idea how to grieve. From the age of eight, my obsession with death prevented me from attending wakes and funerals without becoming literally sick. I did of course attend my father's services in spite of that fear. All I remember is that I cried through the entire wake and funeral. I had no idea what was happening inside of me except that I was filled with grief and had no idea how to manage it. I could actually feel my heart aching, and crying was the only release. I felt totally embarrassed at the services because of what I considered my lack of control. As I perceived it, I was the only person unloading my tears in public. I was haunted by the question "Why am I so weak?" I was comparing my grief to the grief of others, something I have learned not to do. I had no idea that it was perfectly normal to cry in public when experiencing loss, I had no idea that I was expressing my grief in the only way I knew, and I didn't realize that the accumulation of past losses, which I had not grieved, was assaulting me as well.

Fortunately, my husband and family were supportive of me and, at the time, I had recently joined a twelve-step program. I met many wonderful people who helped me to cope and, by the power of their example, they taught me how to love myself and how to live a better life. I continued on my trip of self-discovery for many years, but looking back I realize that all the losses I had encountered in my life were well packed and stored away deep within me, so deep that I had no idea they were there. And so I continued to experience grief and I continued to deal with it by taking care of everyone else but myself, the same way I dealt with my sister's death and all the losses that followed. If you ever need a distraction from yourself, caretaking is the answer. It's an around-the-clock job with no benefits except that it keeps you estranged from your sadness. And all the grief gets put on the back burner and you are deceived into believing that only time will heal it. After my father died, I took on the responsibility of my mother. I did not truly grieve my loss; I simply did what I was best at—I buried it with busyness.

It has been many years, but I still miss my father and I expect I always will. I still love Marigolds, nature, and animals as he did. I truly regret that when he died I was aware only of the painful state of grief that was created by his separation from me. I did not deal with the loss because I had no awareness of the grieving process. I simply continued living my life for others, trying to fix them and to keep them happy. I lived in a state of busyness, stressful busyness, not the type of busy that involves having fun and living a healthy life but the kind of busy that creates the energy needed to continue fixing problems in order to feel alive. I not only buried my father, I buried my feelings of sadness and loss over his death. Unfortunately, feelings buried alive have a way of releasing themselves in the form chronic stress. Regretfully, I was unaware of the process of grieving at the time of my father's death, and the feelings of grief continued to accumulate as I continued to live with a broken spirit.

Mother's Day

Agnes Sharpe Mahar
March 13, 1901 - May 8, 1994

Life without my mother was unimaginable to me. I had been attached to her since I could remember, and I had no concept of

Mary Croft

life without her. After her death on Mother's Day in 1994, I was devastated. My insides felt hollow, empty; on the outside I felt very fragile as if I would crumble if someone touched me. Fortunately, I had been experimenting with the grieving process, so I made a conscious effort to deal with my loss.

My mother's youth was interesting to me, and, being the great storyteller that she was, she kept me in

awe with the tales of her childhood. My favorite is the story of her picking coal at the local railroad yard, ironically, the station at which my father eventually worked. "It wasn't unusual for kids to do that in those days," my mother would assure me. She and her siblings would gather the "best" pieces of coal that had fallen off the trains and bring them home to her mother to heat the house. One day she climbed so high on the coal pile that she couldn't get down and had to be rescued by the Providence Fire Department. It was difficult for me to imagine my mother being in such a dangerous position.

Then there was the story about my mother's tonsillectomy. Because my grandmother had other children at home, a neighbor offered to transport my mother to

the hospital for the operation. Cars were a rare commodity in those days so my mother and her neighbor set out for the hospital with my mother's red wagon as transport. My mother had been told by a friend that the sheet my grandmother handed her as she left would be necessary because of all the blood she would lose, so she was terrified. On her way to the hospital she began plotting her escape from surgery. As they neared the hospital, she jumped out of the wagon, sheet still in hand, and ran home. And so the happy ending to the story was, "And I still have my tonsils." That was my mother!

As an adolescent, my mother dreamed of becoming a nurse. In those days, the requirements were that you had to be an eighth-grade graduate, age fourteen or more, and you had to purchase your own uniform. That would have been a breeze if my mother's family hadn't been poor. Her grandmother, who was very supportive and kind to my mother, offered to buy the uniform when my mother graduated in June of that year so that she could pursue her dream. It sounded like a good plan to my mother as she waited in anticipation of the day. A short while before her fourteenth birthday arrived, her mother promised that there would be a present waiting for her on the big day. My mother was very excited, of course, and surprised because, as she said, "We never got presents in those days." On March 13, 1915, my mother turned fourteen and my grandmother announced to her that she had found her a job working in a factory. That was her present and that was the end of her dream, as well. I could cry every time I think of my mother's disappointment.

My mother made it very clear that her brother, James, who was a driver for the open-air-trolleys that served the Eagle Park section of Providence, was her pride and joy. She spoke of him often and with great admiration. When he became ill, my mother was devastated. Because he had served in the United States Navy,

Mary Croft

he was taken to the Newport Naval Hospital for treatment. In spite of being pregnant, my mother travelled by bus to Newport every day to spend time with him. Such a devoted woman my mother was!

Although she tried to assure me that her childhood was a happy one, I knew my mother's family was poor and that she had been deprived of affection as a result of losing her father at a young age. And I knew her brother's death had a profound effect on her life as well because I could sense her deep sadness whenever she

Letters to Barbara

spoke of him. I felt responsible for my mother's unhappiness and I tried desperately to make it up to her. Such a heavy burden I placed upon myself.

My mother married my father on June 29, 1918. She was seventeen and he was twenty-seven. They raised five children together, my father worked seven days a week on the railroad, and my mother was a stay-at-home mother. I never remember feeling deprived in any way. Although we weren't rich, we always had what we needed. My mother was an excellent money manager and a good cook, and my father was hard working. They provided their children with a sense of security and created a safe environment in which we all grew. Home was my haven, I felt extremely safe there.

It was a busy household with relatives and friends visiting often. People felt welcome there, and there was always room at the table for one more, or two, or three, or more. I have memories from my early childhood of sharing Thanksgiving and Christmas dinners with World War II servicemen who were stationed in Rhode Island. My sister, Dorothy, worked as a photographer in Providence, at the time, and servicemen would visit the store to have their photographs taken. My parents were very grateful for the hospitality shown to my brother, Thomas, by families in England and France where he was stationed; and, to pay it forward, they allowed my sister to invite the servicemen to our home for holiday meals. Barbara and I loved the attention we received from our guests, and I'm sure our guests were impressed by our showing-off under the guise of entertaining them. I think it made their holiday a bit more enjoyable, too. My parents were generous people who, by their example, taught me the meaning of kindness and sharing.

As I said, in our home there was always plenty of room at the table. My brother, Thomas, after he was married and had a family of his own, stopped in every morning for breakfast. Like my father, he worked on the railroad; however, he worked the night shift and got home about 7:30 am. Fortunately, he lived in close proximity to us, making it easy for him to make the stop at our house for breakfast each morning before returning home. I looked forward to our conversations over breakfast, and I admired my parents for creating a home where everyone felt welcomed.

After my sister died, my mother seemed to focus most of her attention on me. My sister, Dorothy, and my brother, Thomas, both got married shortly after Barbara

Letters to Barbara

died. My brother, James, was in college and living on-campus which sort of put me in the category of being raised as an only child. That, and the fear that accompanied my mother's loss of Barbara, probably set the stage for the intense bond that developed between us. As I said, I felt very responsible for her happiness. That's just the way it was. We formed a dependency on each other, and as the years passed I lived in fear of the day she would die. And when that day finally arrived on Mother's Day, 1994, I felt like an emotional orphan.

My mother was a good woman, strong in her beliefs and not easily swayed. People looked up to her and admired her strong character. She was sought after by family, neighbors, and friends for advice and counsel because of her wisdom. She was selfless when it came to family, always giving without expecting in return. She was an easy person to love, but she was a very private person, never expressing her feelings, never crying aloud. As a result, I considered it a weakness that I was an extremely sensitive and emotional person, unlike my mother. Fortunately, I have come to accept my sensitivity as a strength rather than a weakness, a trait that enables me to empathize with others as well as myself, a trait that allows me to accept my grief as an extremely significant part of my life, a trait that makes it possible for me to outwardly grieve my losses without feeling embarrassed and inadequate.

My mother was well-liked and had not one enemy that I can recall. She prided herself in the statement, "I never hated anyone in my entire life." My children who were reared to freely express themselves, negative as well as positive emotions, found my mother's claim difficult to believe, so difficult that they spent a great deal of time interrogating her and trying to get her to admit that she had, in fact, hated at least once in her lifetime. They were totally unsuccessful, and I might say frustrated, in their plight. My mother stood her ground as she did with all her beliefs, "I never hated anyone." was her adamant response. She was an extremely proud woman.

Through the years, my mother was an enjoyable presence in our family and I knew that life would never be the same after she died. She was the matriarch, the keeper, the presence at every function. My children and grandchildren adored her.

As she aged, her health declined and my daily life began to revolve around her. My husband, my sister,

Letters to Barbara

Dorothy, and I provided the physical support she needed in order to maintain her own home and to live independently. Her life-long wish was, "I never want to be a burden to my children." And so, on Mother's Day in 1994, at the age of ninety-three, she died in her own home surrounded by her family.

As I said earlier, I felt like an emotional orphan the day my mother died, and I couldn't imagine my world without her. Fortunately, I had made some progress with processing my grief. Although I had no idea how I would manage, I believed that I could.

I reached out to family and friends, I joined a bereavement group, and, yes, I cried without feeling like a weakling! I utilized my travel time to and from work as my "cry time." It helped because it provided the release I needed and it didn't interfere with anyone else's day. I gathered as much information as I could about losing a parent. One of the things that helped me to endure the pain was reading that the loss of one's mother could be the most spiritually growthful experience in a lifetime, the most painful but the most growthful. It made me realize that I simply needed to identify my sadness, to accept my grief, and to use the process of grieving in order to grow spiritually and live healthily.

Mary Croft

Every Sunday my husband and I visited my mother's grave and placed a rose on it, I shared memories of her lifetime with family and friends, I wrote letters in my journal to my sister about my feelings. I even forced myself to have fun when I wasn't in the mood for it. One of the benefits of having children and grandchildren is that you share many of the same memories. In my case, because my mother had been close to all of us, we had many memories of her to share.

Shortly after my mother died, my sister and I purchased a plaque in her memory. It sits among others in a beautiful park in Point Judith where my sister spent her summers. It's a beautiful spot which was dedicated by the owner to the memory of his own mother, a place where families can go for picnics and where, on a nice day, you can sit, overlooking the ocean, and watch the surfers ride the waves. A beautiful place to memorialize a life!

Almost immediately after my mother died, I felt an urgency to preserve all her photos. I spent hours sorting through them, putting them in some form of chronological order, and labeling them. I then had them transferred to a disc for safe-keeping. I cried throughout the entire project; but, when it was completed, I felt as if my mother's life had been memorialized! I gave a copy to each of my siblings.

Mary Croft

Grieving my way through the picture project gave me a great deal of time to think about my relationship with my mother. What did I miss the most about her? What did she mean to me? What did our relationship signify? How different would life be without her? What need did she fulfill in me? These questions and their answers made me aware that, if I wanted to fill the space that my mother's death created in my life, I would have to be to myself what she had been to me. I would have to be a mother to myself. I would have to do for myself what she had done for me. And so, I learned to love myself as my mother loved me, I learned to listen to myself as she listened to me, I learned to be a friend to

Letters to Barbara

myself as she was to me. I've learned to take care of myself, to encourage myself and not judge myself, and to sing my own praises. As I do these things for myself, I think of my mother and the influence she had on my life, and I think of the growth I've experienced as the result of grieving her death. Thank you so much, Agnes Sharpe Mahar, for being the wonderful mother and grandmother you were!

Nancy

11/12/1961 – 9/23/2006

My dear daughter, Nancy Croft, was born on the evening of November 12, 1961, at Woman and Infants Hospital in Providence, Rhode Island. She was a beautiful baby, born perfectly healthy. Weighing 9 lb. 1 oz. made her look like a three-month-old. Her hair, what little she had, was strawberry blonde in color. Her eyes were blue like mine. She talked very early and she walked at ten months of age. She was a good-natured baby with a quiet docile temperament.

Letters to Barbara

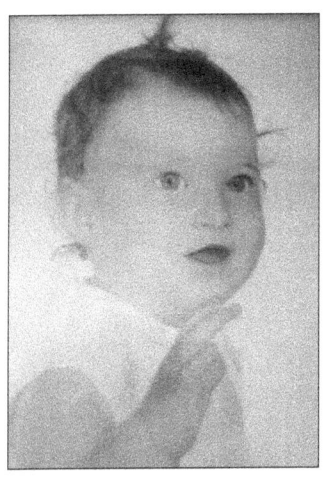

Looking back, I think Nancy was deprived of her babyhood. When she was only one-year-old I gave birth to her brother, John, and her sister, Mary, was only two and a half at the time. Three children under the age of two and a half, with two in diapers, was difficult for me. I felt like I needed an extra set of hands. I think she did not get as much attention as she needed because I had to spread myself so thinly. Mother's guilt!

Nancy and her younger brother were my Irish twins. I had wanted to have twins, but this was the closest I came to it. Because they were born a year apart, they shared a closeness to each other that remained in adulthood. Nancy taught John everything she knew, how to ride a bike, how to tie his shoes, and how to pronounce his "esses" without lisping. These are just a few of the fond memories he cherishes of their relationship.

Nancy and her older sister, Mary, were constant playmates because of their closeness in age. They rode bikes together, they took dance classes together, and they walked to school together every day. When they weren't in school, they played school. Of course, big sister was always the teacher. Nancy looked up to her older sister and assumed the role of doing whatever she was told to do. It sort of backfired the day that "Doctor

Letters to Barbara

Mary" told "Patient Nancy" to put a vitamin pill up her nose (they were three and four years old) and it got lodged in her nostril. Today, we laugh when we reminisce about the incident but, at the time, we couldn't appreciate the humor in it.

Nancy was eight years old when her younger sister, Regina, was born and so she assumed a protective role with her. She took her baby sister to have her ears pierced, she let her drive the car before she was of driving age, and, after hearing that some students were bullying Regina, she showed up at the junior high school to lend her support.

Mary Croft

Although their relationships were different, each of Nancy's siblings cherishes what they shared with her and each has had to grieve in their own personal way.

Nancy generated warmth. When she gave a hug, it was truly a hug. You could feel her spirit as well as her body, and you knew that she loved you. It was fun to be around her. Her personality was dynamic and she enjoyed laughing and making others laugh. Whenever we are together, we share stories about the funny things she said and did. We each have our own favorite stories and they seem to find their way into most of our conversations.

As a child, Nancy was very attached to me; and, although it took on a different form, that attachment continued throughout her adult life. I struggled with this issue and I tried to make changes, but my guilt and fear prevented me from totally letting go. I knew by that time that I couldn't fix her problems but, as a mother, I felt a moral obligation to try. To do nothing created an avalanche of emotions in me with which I could not deal.

Nancy died unexpectedly on September 23, 2006. The worst possible tragedy happened to me that day, and, in an instant, my life was changed. For years I had

Letters to Barbara

feared for her life, but when the news came I was shocked. It's difficult to explain the feeling but I knew that my life would never be the same.

It was a dismal day, not actually raining, but gray. I was hobbling around on crutches, having had foot surgery the previous day. I heard the doorbell ring and then I heard my husband talking to someone in the living room. When I entered the room, the look on John's face immediately signaled that something was wrong. When I heard him cry out "Oh, no! God, no!" I knew someone had died. I experienced a sensation of panic and I wanted to deny my own existence; instead, within seconds, the news of my daughter's death became a tragic reality. I screamed!

Mary Croft

Family members rushed to my side, but I was inconsolable. I felt numb and anxious at the same time, and my heart ached for Nancy's children, Sarah and Justin.

When the services were over, I wondered how I would survive without my daughter. I couldn't picture life without her. I knew she had left a part of herself with me, but I also knew that she had taken a big part of me with her. I wasn't sure I could go on. I wasn't sure I wanted to go on. Fortunately, I knew that these feelings were perfectly normal, that I wasn't going crazy, and that, with the help of God, I would do my best to

Letters to Barbara

grieve my loss by using the process I had spent years practicing and studying.

Again, I joined a bereavement group and shared my grief with the compassionate people there. As a family, we memorialized Nancy's life by putting together a memory garden. We planted a tree, some flowery shrubs, and different colored flowers. We included a few meaningful plaques, a cross, and a flag, all the things that were special to her. In the summertime, the morning glories climb to the top of the hummingbird feeder. Their buds, closing at dusk and opening again in the morning, are reminders to me that, although there is death, there is also rebirth. The garden is a symbol of Nancy's love of nature and provides many fond memories of the times we spent together.

Mary Croft

Nancy is physically gone but in spirit she lives among us. I see her in every flower, I hear her in every song, and I feel her presence each day. Every morning I put on a spray of her favorite cologne and I think of how much she loved when I wore it.

I long to touch my daughter again, I yearn to hug her. I am reminded each day that grieving her death is a never-ending process and will continue for as long as I live. I will always miss her, I will always cry when I think of her, and I will never get over the grief I feel about losing her. But today I know that it's okay to feel that way, that there is no time limit when it comes to grieving and that it can go on forever. People said I

Letters to Barbara

changed after Nancy died, that I wasn't myself. I knew my life wasn't the same, but how could it be? Why should it be? I lost a part of myself that day, and there is no way of erasing that loss. No amount of time, no words, no tools will ever bring enough relief from that pain.

Although I must live without the physical presence of Nancy, I attempt to find ways in which to continue my spiritual bond with her. Her death has put me on a long journey through a very dark tunnel; and, although grief led me to that tunnel, the grieving process navigates me through it. I have never gotten over the loss of my daughter, but because of my knowledge of grief and grieving, I have been able to live in spite of it.

Mary Croft

The tragedy of losing my child weighs heavy on my soul, because I know that the times we spent together, her sense of humor, her child-like love for me, her warmth and caring for others, all this and more, will never decorate my life again. Rest in peace, dear Nancy.

Letters to Barbara

Good Grief

Good grief simply means that, instead of denying or burying our losses, we identify them, we accept that they're causing our grief, and we take action in order to work through them. Although it's not easy to work through grief, the benefits outweigh the risks. Grieving our losses can free us and promote our spiritual growth. Attempting to run away from grief is not the answer because the feelings will undoubtedly return to haunt you! To deny your grief is to pretend it doesn't exist; to bury your grief by turning it inward is to delay the pain or to experience it in psychosomatic ways as I did. Actively grieving our losses enhances our well-being, and we can become transformed by it rather than becoming paralyzed by it. We can choose our own paths by using good grief.

Keep in mind that death, although it is the ultimate loss, is not the only cause of grief. Our losses occur daily and are on a continuum from minor to major. Loss can be as simple as losing a tooth or as major as the death of a loved one or a pet. The way in which we deal with our losses determines the effect they have on us. Losses have personalities of their own and are an integral part of who we are. They can make us feel tired, angry, sad, depressed, anxious, or lonesome; in other words they affect us in a negative way. They interfere with our happiness unless we grieve them.

Do not allow your losses to deceive you. Connect with them, try to label them. This can be difficult at times especially when the losses are subtle in nature. After many years of exploring grief, I realized that many of my losses had been the result of disappointments, disappointments because of the false perceptions I entertained of myself, of others, and of life in general. How many times had I been disappointed when I discovered that I wasn't nearly as important to another person as I had thought? How many times had my expectations of myself and others been too high? How often had I entertained the thought that everyone was sincere in their behavior and that they truly meant what they said? Life is good, but life is about being human. We all disappoint ourselves and others at some point, but it's important to recognize the disappointments as losses so that we can grieve them.

The process of good grief is task-oriented. Simply stated, one needs to identify loss, accept that it is causing feelings of grief, and work through it in an effective way. In other words, be vigilant about loss and the grief it causes. Be proactive and accept that, although you are powerless over the loss, you are not powerless over your reaction to it. Good grief can be an opportunity to grow. Face it, accept it, and grow from it. Consider it a gift to yourself to engage in the process that can journey you to a place of acceptance and even contentment. You are defined by your feelings, so don't run away from them. Don't be fooled by your grief. The clue is that grief makes you feel poorly; it causes negative feelings and robs you of your peace of mind. It causes stress and distress. Find a way to recognize this connection between your losses and your grief and develop ways to get it outside of yourself. Make good grief

Letters to Barbara

a major part of your journey by allowing it to enter your busy day. Make room for it, you won't be sorry!

Make it a daily habit to reflect on your losses, and connect them to your feelings of grief. Gift yourself with some quality time each day to ponder your feelings so that you can connect them to the minor as well as the major losses that you experience. I prefer to label my losses because it gives me a better understanding of them, and I'm the type of person who likes to know what makes the clock tick!

Accept your losses and connect them to the grief you are experiencing. Know that it is a normal reaction to feel uncomfortable when there is loss. Give yourself permission to feel the way you feel. Don't minimize the loss and don't compare your grief to the grief others feel. Grief is like fingerprints—no two are the same. It's a personal matter; there are no "shoulds" or "shouldn'ts" when it comes to the subject of feelings. They are what they are, and the way we deal with them is part of who we are as a person. Talk about them, write about them, draw pictures, do whatever it takes to get them outside of yourself and into the open where you can get a better view of them. Don't allow them to accumulate and take up precious space in your emotional memory bank. Save that room for more positive thoughts.

Use your creativity. Once you form the habit of recognizing and accepting your grief, you will be able to empower yourself by taking action, by healing and growing, and changing. Because we are individuals, the process is different from one person to another. It's best to tailor the formula to your own needs. Connecting and dialoguing with people seems to give me a better perspective on my emotions and allows me to be more objective about them. Just knowing that another person accepts them makes is easier for me to do the same. There's something to be said about comradery here!

It's important to be selective and to connect with people who will listen without judging you. Choose someone with an open mind and a certain degree of compassion and empathy. A conversation with a good listener is a blessing and can validate your feelings of grief. Find someone in whom you can confide and trust. Remember that this is new to you and that you are dealing with sensitive material, so be gentle with yourself. By sharing your grief, you will become more aware of the situations that affect you, you will accept them more easily, and you will be more inclined to use the grieving process.

Although grief can make us feel anti-social, it's therapeutic to be around others when you are feeling vulnerable. Socialize even if you don't feel up to it. It makes sense that, when we feel loss, we have been disconnected from someone or something and that there is no way to replace that person or thing in our lives. Making other connections and sharing our feelings about the loss can help to fill the void it has created. Socializing might seem like an unreasonable task at a time when you feel like crawling under a rock, when you feel as if every ounce of energy has left your body, when you just don't give a hoot about anything; however, it's at this point that you need to be firm with yourself. Convince yourself that connecting with other people is grief work and that the payoff is worth the energy and discipline it requires.

Bereavement groups are extremely helpful when you are facing a major loss. You come together with other people who understand that you are grieving, and it's a safe place to be sad, to feel angry and confused. It's okay to cry there, too. There's nothing unusual about bathing in a pool of your own tears, and it's acceptable there. After my mother's death, I made a slot in my busy day for "cry time," something the bereavement group gave me permission to do. It fit nicely into my commute to and from work and nobody was affected by my tears except those overly curious people who stare into other people's cars while driving. At that point, they didn't matter to me at all, and the crying relieved me. It was good grief!

Writing letters and keeping a journal is an effective form of communication and a healthy way to get your grief outside of yourself. It works with minor losses as well as major ones. Expressing your feelings and concerns on paper, as well as re-reading what you wrote, can provide you with a clearer perspective on your emotions. Keep a journal or writing tablet next to your bed. It works wonders for me on sleepless nights.

Speaking of journals, I recently went on a trip to Alabama to visit grandchildren. The trip was number one on my bucket list, so I was feeling very excited about it. I couldn't wait to see them. I didn't want to fly, so my granddaughter and her fiancée unselfishly offered to drive me. While we were planning the road trip, I could feel the fear creeping up on me, a fear that had prevented me from engaging in sleepovers as a

Letters to Barbara

child, a fear that stopped me from venturing away from home on many occasions. I began to connect my fear to feelings of loss, loss of time spent with my husband and children, loss of my familiar surroundings, loss of my comfort zone. Grief was on its rampage and about to take over again! I was determined that my grief would not spoil the trip for myself and the others, and I was determined to have the best time possible and to see that they did as well. Fortunately, I realized that I needed a plan! While I was packing, I happened to find a journal that was given to me by a friend. It found its way into my carry-bag for future use, and off we went, the three of us and my journal. We weren't very far from home when the negative thoughts started. Will I be able to do this? Will everything be okay at home? Will my husband get sick? Will my homesickness spoil the trip? Should I have done this? The self-doubt was setting in so I took out my red leather-bound book and started writing. I was grateful I had taken the journal, because it provided an outlet for me to look straight into the eyes of my grief and to deal with it by putting it outside of myself. I was able to make the trip without spoiling their time and mine. My fears were alleviated and I was able to put a check mark on my bucket list when it was over. By the way, everything was fine when I arrived back in Rhode Island.

It's amazing how writing can be so helpful in getting things outside of yourself. Although I prefer dialoguing, there are times when the opportunity is not available and writing becomes the alternative tool. The information can always be shared with a friend or confidant at a later date. Journaling is good grief!

Be patient with your grief. Try not to put a time-limit on it. Grieving takes as long as it takes. And please don't pay attention to the well-meaning people who say, "But it's been a while now, hasn't it?" or "You need to put it behind you now." We are individuals with unique personalities and each has their own sense of timing and rhythm so don't let anyone rush you through your grief! It doesn't work! The healing may take longer for some of us than others. With some losses there is no closure, just transformation. I have come to accept that the loss of my daughter will never be over. Why would it be? Why should it be? A part of me died that day, and, although I will heal enough to continue my journey, my life will never be the same without her.

Letters to Barbara

Loss is personal, grief is personal, and so it is with grieving. Be patient with the process and allow yourself the time it takes.

Every picture tells a story, so is it any wonder that many people, adults as well as children, get relief from their art work. My long-time friend, Betty, who also uses writing as a tool, finds great relief from drawing. She has produced some awesome art work by utilizing this form of creative expression. When you grieve, it doesn't matter which tool you use; the important thing is to work the process so that your feelings are outside of yourself. Creativity is your friend when you are grieving. There are many tools to use, so be an explorer and try them all until you find your niche.

Mary Croft

Memorializing your major losses is a form of good grief and an opportunity to use your creativity. You can find different ways to honor the person's life and to keep their spirit alive as well. When my mother died, the memorial was the photo project, and when my daughter died it was the memory garden. Memorializing a major loss is an opportunity to continue your spiritual bond with the person by preserving your fond memories of them. Be creative, invent a style, and build a long-term memory. This is a form of good grief!

As I was writing *Letters to Barbara* I began to see that, over the years, I was so accustomed to feeling depressed, I had failed to recognize many losses. The losses accumulated and hid like shadows in my mind. Then they would rear their ugly faces when least expected and cause me grief, grief that interfered with the quality of my physical, mental, and spiritual well-being because I didn't recognize it and was confused by it. Journaling made me realize the value of exploring my grief on a daily basis and of taking care of business as it occurred.

Presently, due to the ageing process, I find myself grieving the loss of strength, mobility, and endurance. Although I feel mentally better than I have felt in my entire life, the mere fact that I am getting older causes physical changes in me and those changes cause me grief. I am wiser, more humble, and I have a great faith in God. I've come to the place where I want only what I need and no longer require what I want, and that brings me peace. I have a husband who loves me, I have children and grandchildren who value and respect me, and my general health is very good for my age; however, my physical strength has decreased and my activity level is more restricted by that. I try to be vigilant of these changes and to grieve the feelings of loss that are associated with them. Without the awareness and acceptance of my grief, I would be tricked into believing that my emotions were the result of depression and that there was nothing I could do about my situation. Instead, I have chosen to practice good grief and to process my feelings in some creative way. It will not change my situation, but it will again lead me through the darkness to the light at the end of another tunnel.

As you navigate through the process of practicing good grief, you, too, will make more connections between your negative emotions and the losses that evoke them. Try not to cherry-pick your losses, pay equal attention to all of them. Grieve them, however insignificant they seem to be. Loss is loss, it only matters that you deal with it in a healthy way.

In summary, good grief is knowing, feeling, and doing! Begin to know your losses, let yourself feel the grief, and do something about it. Turn your grief into something positive, let it be a learning experience, and grow from it. Enhance your well-being by inviting good grief into your life and by allowing the grieving process to map your course from loss to freedom. Happy journey!

Letters to Barbara

Examples

I loved Grampa so much I could squeeze him. My mother said he used to pick me up from my crib and show me off to everybody. He always let me look through the things he was saving. He saved everything. He was so nice and he loved me. He passed away.

--- a page from a book dictated by six year-old Regina who grieved her grandfather's death.

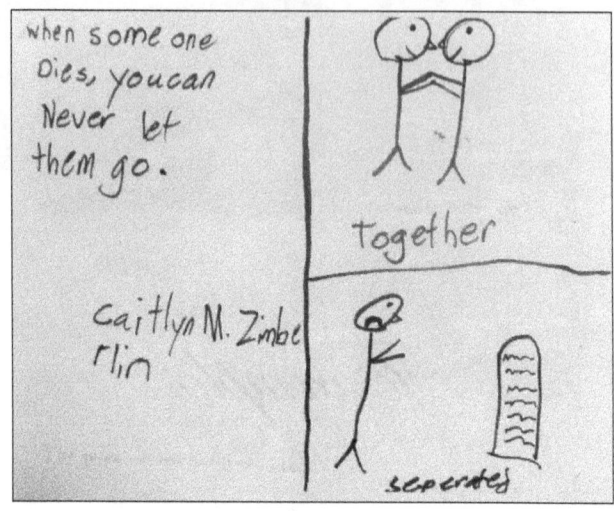

Above and below: a niece grieving her aunt.

Letters to Barbara

> Dear Grandma Mahar,
>
> I love you and miss you. I was wondering if you were having a good time in heaven. It is summer. In September I'll be in 4th grade can you believe it? I think you can. I know you can not write back to me. I wanted to write to you. I love you and hope you are looking down on me.
>
> Your grand Daughter
>
> Sarah Swanson
>
> I love you with all my heart

A granddaughter grieving her grandmother.

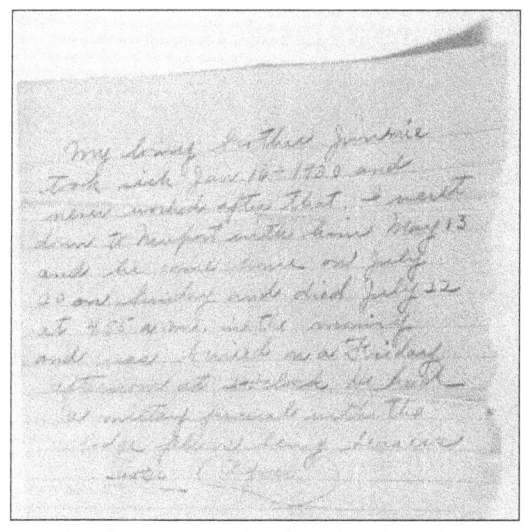

And a sister grieving her brother.

Mary Croft

Thank You

With Sincere Gratitude to:

My husband and my children,

And my grandchildren.

Letters to Barbara

About the Author

Mary Croft describes herself as a late bloomer and a woman of many roles. After enjoying the 60's as a stay-at-home wife and mother, she went back to college and eventually began her career, working full time in the field of special education and part time in the area of substance abuse. She received her bachelor's degree from Rhode Island College at the age of fifty-nine. Although she has always entertained the thought of writing professionally, it wasn't until she reached her seventies that publishing her first book, *Letters to Barbara*, became a reality.

www.ingramcontent.com/pod-product-compliance
Lightning Source LLC
Chambersburg PA
CBHW071131090426
42736CB00012B/2091